ESSENTIAL ELEMENTS®

GUITAR ENSEMBLES

GREAT THEMES

CONTENTS

Arrangements by Chip Henderson

ISBN 978-1-61780-757-2

HAL•LEONARD®
CORPORATION

7777 W. BLUEMOUND RD. P.O. BOX 13819 MILWAUKEE, WI 53213

Visit Hal Leonard Online at
www.halleonard.com

ADDAMS FAMILY THEME
Theme from the TV Show and Movie
Music and Lyrics by Vic Mizzy

*Finger snaps or muted strums.

C

THEME FROM E.T.
(The Extra-Terrestrial)
from the Universal Picture E.T. (THE EXTRA-TERRESTRIAL)

Music by John Williams

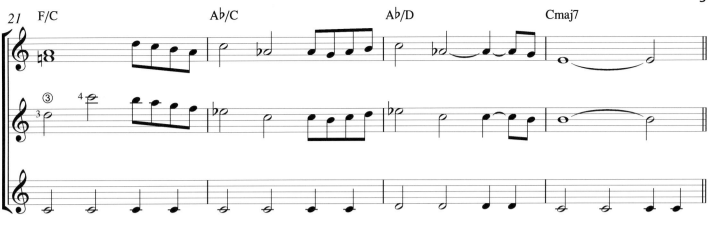

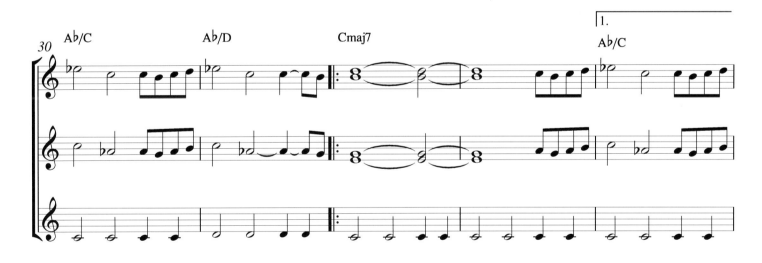

FORREST GUMP - MAIN TITLE
(Feather Theme)
from the Paramount Motion Picture FORREST GUMP
Music by Alan Silvestri

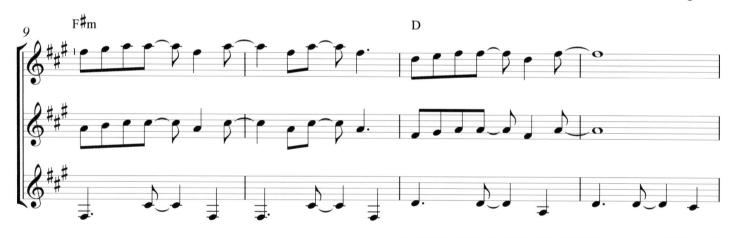

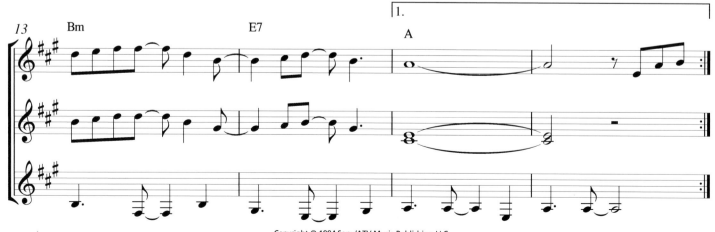

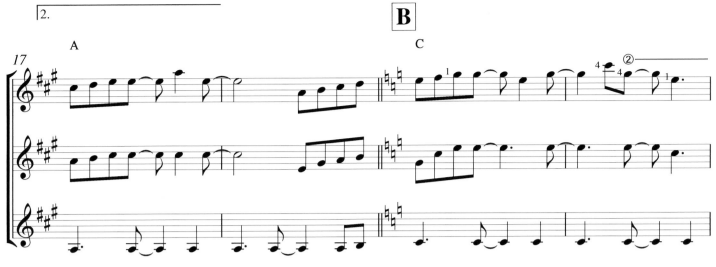

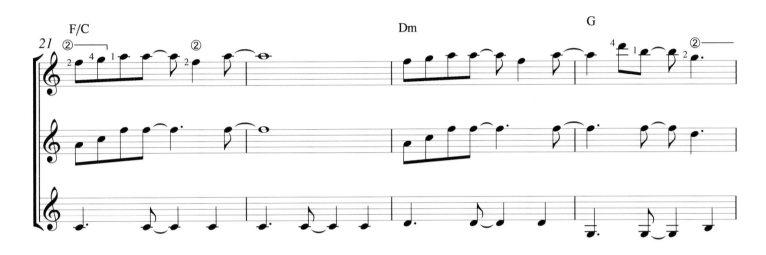

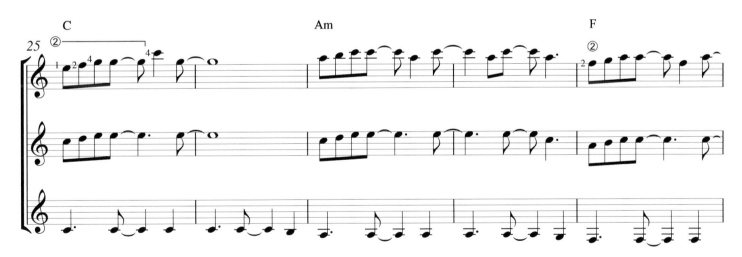

THE GODFATHER
(Love Theme)
from the Paramount Picture THE GODFATHER
By Nino Rota

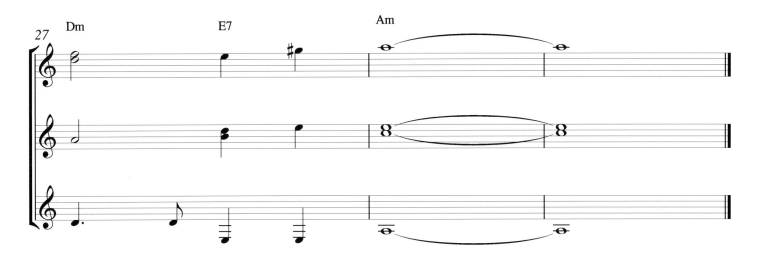

HAWAII FIVE-O THEME

from the Television Series

By Mort Stevens

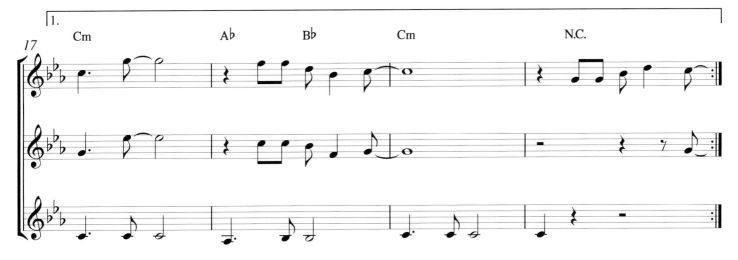

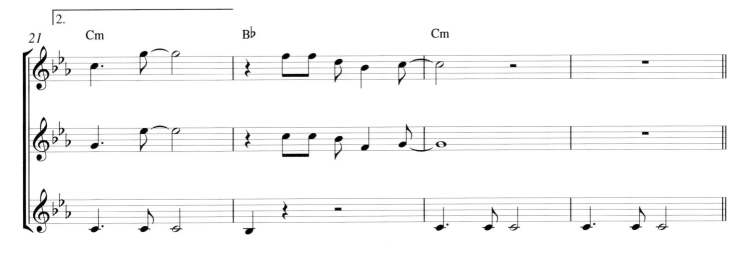

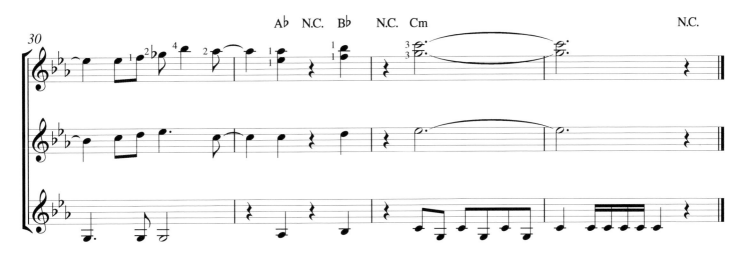

LINUS AND LUCY

By Vince Guaraldi

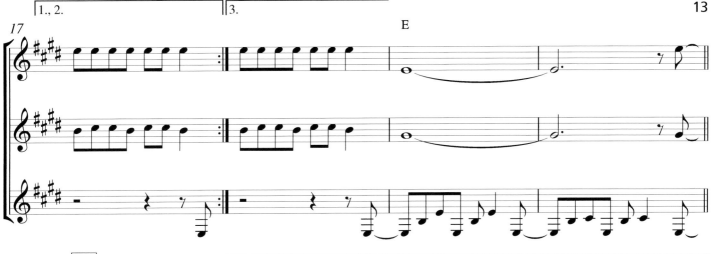

THE MASTERPIECE
the TV Theme from MASTERPIECE THEATRE

By J.J. Mouret and Paul Parnes

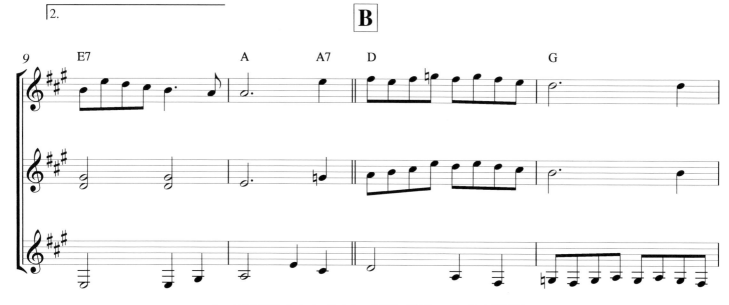

MISSION: IMPOSSIBLE THEME

from the Paramount Television Series MISSION: IMPOSSIBLE

By Lalo Schifrin

To Coda ⊕

D.C. al Coda

⊕ Coda

THE MUNSTERS THEME

from the Television Series

By Jack Marshall

THE MUPPET SHOW THEME

from the Television Series

Words and Music by Jim Henson and Sam Pottle

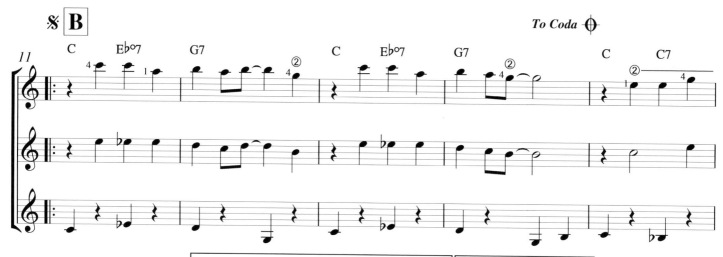

C

D.S. al Coda

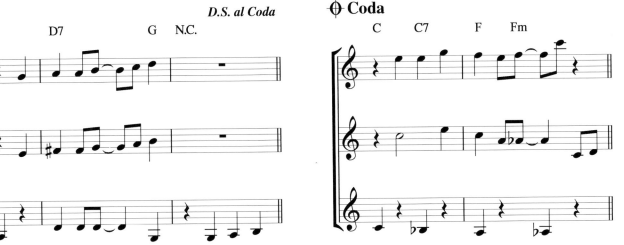

Coda

D

PETER GUNN
Theme Song from The Television Series

By Henry Mancini

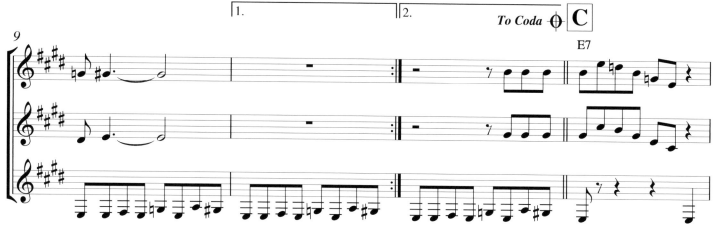

D.S. al Coda
(take repeat)

Coda

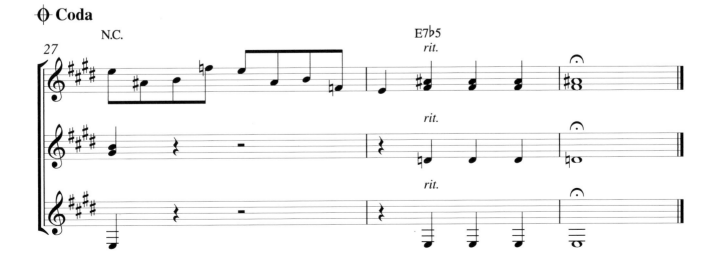

THE PINK PANTHER

from THE PINK PANTHER

By Henry Mancini

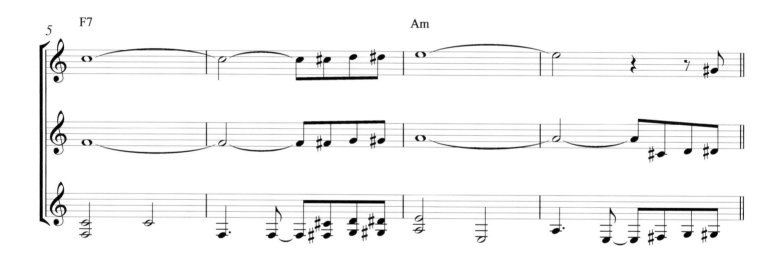

THEME FROM SPIDER MAN

Written by Bob Harris and Paul Francis Webster

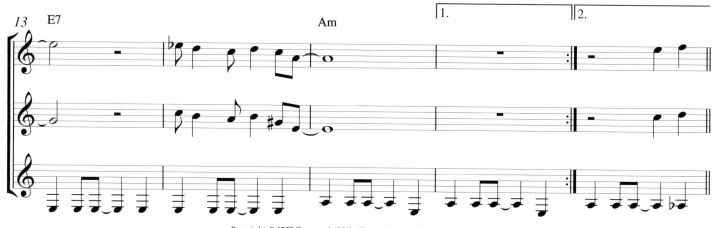

C

D.S. al Coda

Coda

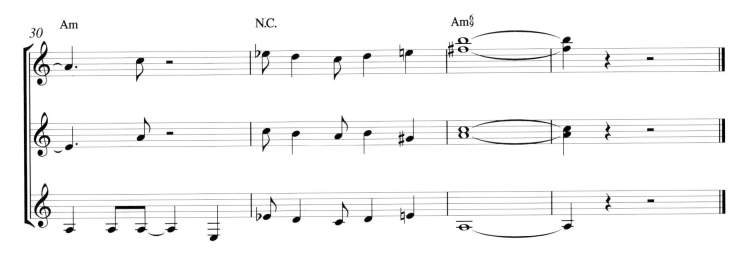

THEME FROM "STAR TREK®"

from the Paramount Television Series STAR TREK

Words by Gene Roddenberry
Music by Alexander Courage

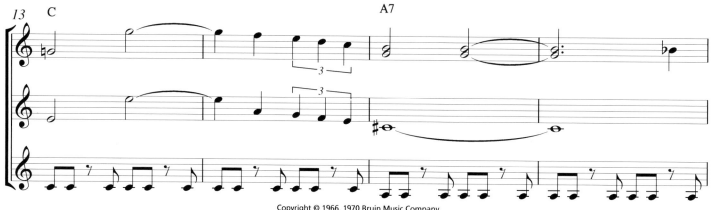

D.S. al Coda

⊕ Coda

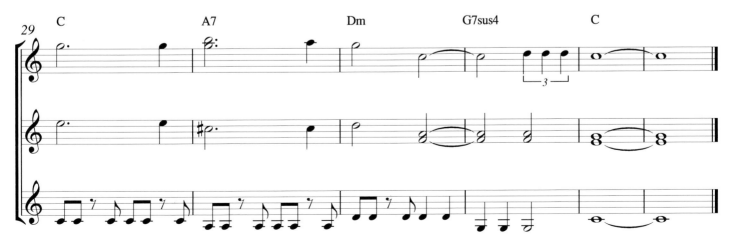

HE'S A PIRATE

**from Walt Disney Pictures' PIRATES OF THE CARIBBEAN:
THE CURSE OF THE BLACK PEARL**

Music by Klaus Badelt

D.S. al Coda
(take repeat)

Coda

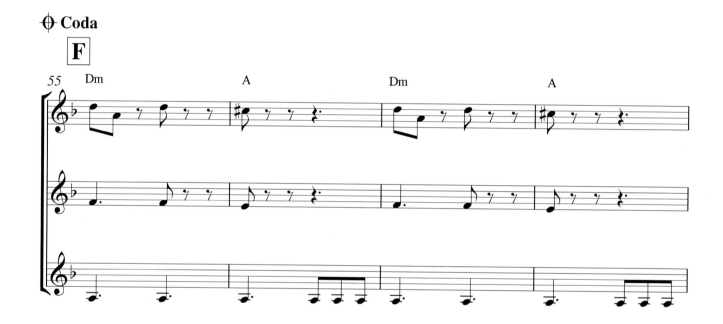

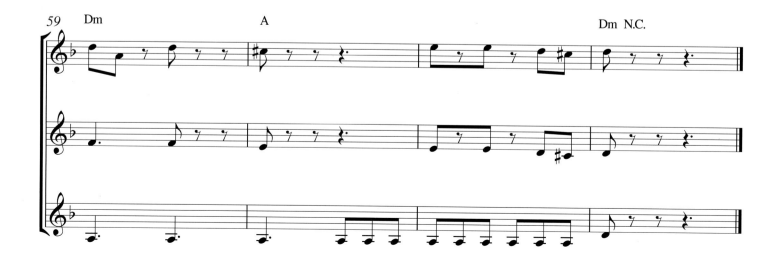